Surviving HURRICANE KATRINA

Surviving Disaster:
Real-Life Tales of Survival and Resilience

Kira Freed

rosen publishing's
rosen
central®

New York

Published in 2016 by The Rosen Publishing Group, Inc.
29 East 21st Street, New York, NY 10010

Copyright © 2016 by The Rosen Publishing Group, Inc.

First Edition

Developed and produced for Rosen by BlueApple*Works* Inc.

Art Director: T.J. Choleva

Managing Editor for BlueApple*Works*: Melissa McClellan
Designer: Joshua Avramson
Photo Research: Jane Reid
Editor: Marcia Abramson

Photo Credits: © Bob Moeinian (p. 35); Keystone Press: © Chris Zuppa (p. 16); Public Domain: U.S. Air Force photo by Master Sergeant Michael E. Best (Cover); NOAA (p. 6); NASA (p. 8); U.S Navy Photo/PH2 RJ Stratchko (p. 12); U.S. Coast Guard, Petty Officer 2nd Class Kyle Niemi (p. 20); U.S. Navy Photo/Airman Jeremy L. Grisham (p. 30); Fema: Jocelyn Augustino (title page, p. 4, 11, 19, 24, 27, 29, 40, 45, back cover); Mark Wolfe (p. 15); Barry Bahler (p. 23); Marvin Nauman (p. 38); Win Henderson (p. 43)

Library of Congress Cataloging-in-Publication Data

Freed, Kira.

Surviving Hurricane Katrina/Kira Freed.—First edition.

    pages cm.—(Surviving disaster)

Includes bibliographical references and index.

ISBN 978-1-4994-3665-5 (library bound)—ISBN 978-1-4994-3667-9 (pbk.)—
ISBN 978-1-4994-3668-6 (6-pack)

1. Hurricane Katrina, 2005—Juvenile literature. 2. Hurricanes—Gulf States—Juvenile literature.
3. Emergency management—Gulf States—Juvenile literature. I. Title.

HV636 2005 .G85 F74 2016

976'.044—dc23

2015002473

Manufactured in the United States of America

Contents

Hurricanes can spread flooding for miles as they travel inland, and floodwaters can continue to rise even after the storm itself has passed.

Chapter 1
Atlantic Hurricane Seasons

If you've ever experienced a hurricane or witnessed the destruction that this type of extreme weather can bring, you're not likely to forget it. Hurricanes are a type of tropical cyclone—a rapidly rotating storm system with high winds, a center of low pressure, and spiral thunderstorms that produce very heavy rain. When these storms, particularly severe ones, occur in the North Atlantic Ocean, they're referred to as hurricanes.

People who live in areas where hurricanes strike know to be on guard for them. Residents of the east coast pay close attention to the Atlantic hurricane season, which officially begins on June 1 and is over by December 1. Although hurricanes can occur outside of these dates, few do. And within this six-month span, 96 percent of major hurricanes occur during the months of August, September, and October.

Between 1966 and 2009, the North Atlantic Ocean, Gulf of Mexico, and Caribbean Sea, collectively referred to as the North Atlantic basin, had an average of 11 tropical cyclones each year, six of which became hurricanes and two of which became major hurricanes.

Storms clouds swirled around Katrina's eye on August 28, 2005. Photos were taken from high-tech planes tracking the storm.

In 2005, this region had more hurricanes than any other year in recorded history. A total of 15 hurricanes occurred that year, seven of which developed into major hurricanes. Two of the seven became the most intense and expensive hurricanes on record.

In 1953, the World Meteorological Association established a procedure for naming tropical storms. Atlantic storms are named sequentially according to the alphabet, with a name starting with the letter A, such as Andrea, being the first tropical storm of the season. (The storms were originally only assigned female names; however, male names were introduced in 1979 and alternate equally with female names.) Names are reused every six years unless a particular storm was so destructive that using its name again would be disturbing to the people affected by it. During 2005, five hurricanes wreaked so much death and destruction that their names have been permanently retired. One of those hurricanes—Katrina—caused unthinkable tragedy, and the millions of people whose lives it directly touched were forever changed.

Measuring Tropical Cyclones

Meteorologists rank tropical cyclones by wind speed. A storm with maximum **sustained** winds of 38 miles per hour (61 kmph) or less is a tropical depression. Between 39 and 73 miles per hour (62–118 kmph), the storm is categorized as a tropical storm. If maximum sustained winds exceed 73 miles per hour (118 kmph), the storm is a hurricane.

The Saffir-Simpson scale categorizes tropical cyclones that have developed into hurricanes.

Category 1	74–95 mph (119–153 kmph)	Some damage
Category 2	96–110 mph (154–177 kmph)	Extensive damage
Category 3	111–129 mph (178–208 kmph)	Devastating damage
Category 4	130–156 mph (209–251 kmph)	**Catastrophic** damage
Category 5	157 mph (252 kmph) or higher	Catastrophic damage

Category 3, 4, and 5 hurricanes are considered major hurricanes.

Katrina barrels toward the Gulf Coast on August 28, 2005, in an image created using photos from a U.S. climate satellite. State borders were added as reference points.

Chapter 2
Hurricane Katrina

When Hurricane Katrina first started to form in mid-August 2005, conditions were typical of weather patterns during the Atlantic hurricane season. The storm originally developed north of Puerto Rico on August 19 and became a tropical depression over the Bahamas on August 23. A band of storm clouds began to form on the north side of the storm's center the following morning. At that point, with wind speeds averaging about 40 miles per hour (65 kmph), the National Hurricane Center reclassified the weather pattern as a tropical storm and named it Katrina.

Wind speeds increased the next day as the storm, now a Category 1 hurricane, made **landfall** in southern Florida during the evening of August 25 with sustained winds of 75 miles per hour (121 kmph). Once Katrina made landfall, it slowed and was downgraded to a tropical storm. Although the hurricane caused 14 deaths in Florida, loss of electrical power to more than a million people, and at least $500 million in property damage, forecasters had no reason to suspect that Katrina would develop into a monster storm.

After leaving Florida on the morning of August 26, Katrina headed southwest out over the Gulf of Mexico. Once there, the storm rapidly grew stronger, reaching sustained wind speeds of close to 100 miles per hour (161 kmph). Late that morning, the National Hurricane Center upgraded it to a Category 2 hurricane and forecast the possibility that Katrina could intensify to Category 4 status within 72 hours. The NHC also forecast a 90 percent likelihood that the storm would hit New Orleans head-on, which could be disastrous since much of the city was below sea level.

As predicted, Katrina grew in strength and was upgraded to a Category 3 hurricane in the early hours of August 27. By midnight, it had become a Category 4 hurricane with sustained winds of 145 miles per hour (233 kmph). The following morning, the storm had developed into a Category 5 hurricane with sustained winds of 175 miles per hour (282 kmph) and wind gusts as high as 215 miles per hour (346 kmph). Not only was Katrina unbelievably strong, but it was also enormous, with hurricane-force winds rotating 105 miles (169 km) out from the center and tropical-force winds extending more than 100 miles (161 km) beyond that.

At this point, Katrina was located about 170 miles (274 km) from the mouth of the Mississippi River. The National Weather Service issued a hurricane warning for the city of New Orleans as well as the northern and southeastern Gulf Coast. The National Hurricane Center described the storm as "potentially catastrophic."

When Katrina struck the Gulf Coast around 7:00 AM on August 29, the storm's winds caused considerable damage, but the aftermath of the hurricane was **calamitous**. High water pushed ashore by Katrina's powerful winds devastated much of the Gulf Coast and caused Lake Pontchartrain's water level to rise. As a result, New Orleans' **levee** system failed, causing severe flooding throughout 80 percent of the city. Power and communications outages, along with slow and poorly coordinated efforts, obstructed the staggering tasks of rescuing people trapped by the water and providing services to thousands stranded in overcrowded shelters. Unimaginable suffering resulted.

About 1,200 people died as a result of Hurricane Katrina and its immediate aftermath. Hundreds of thousands of people were rendered homeless, many permanently, and damage estimates totaled more than $100 billion.

As the floodwaters rose, roads and bridges were washed away in New Orleans.

President George W. Bush met with Louisiana Governor Kathleen Blanco aboard the USS Iwo Jima, which was the command center for relief efforts.

Chapter 3
Preparations for Katrina

Katrina left southern Florida early on August 26 and picked up speed almost immediately over the Gulf of Mexico's warm waters as it headed toward the Gulf Coast. The National Hurricane Center predicted that Katrina would develop into a major hurricane as it moved over the Gulf of Mexico. Louisiana Governor Kathleen Blanco and Mississippi Governor Haley Barbour both declared states of emergency. Governor Blanco also requested that President George W. Bush declare a federal state of emergency in Louisiana, which would free up federal resources to assist during the anticipated crisis. President Bush declared a federal state of emergency in Louisiana the following day.

By early morning on August 27, Katrina had become a Category 3 hurricane large enough to cover the entire Gulf of Mexico. At 2:00 AM on August 28, Katrina was upgraded to Category 4 and, five hours later, to Category 5—the most severe hurricane on the Saffir-Simpson Hurricane Wind Scale. At 10:11 AM, Robert Ricks, forecaster with the National Weather Service, issued a grim statement warning citizens about the severity of the hurricane and the expected devastating damage. Referred to at times as a "doomsday alert," the statement was not taken seriously by many people but proved to be soberingly accurate.

Mayor Ray Nagin issued a **mandatory evacuation** order for New Orleans, and mandatory evacuation orders were also issued for other parts of southern Louisiana as well as low-lying coastal areas of Alabama and Mississippi. President Bush declared a state of emergency in those two states.

With less than a day before Katrina was expected to make landfall, extraordinary measures were required to hasten evacuation. In Louisiana and Mississippi, all lanes on interstate highways were changed to northbound

State of Emergency

A government may declare a state of emergency in the event of a natural or human-caused disaster that threatens public safety. When a state of emergency has been declared, a government may impose certain regulations to protect lives and property. The declaration also provides for resources to address the emergency in the form of money, workers, supplies, and equipment. Under certain conditions, the president has the authority to declare a state of emergency for a state or for the entire country. When this happens, the U.S. Federal Emergency Management Agency (FEMA) is authorized to address the crisis, and federal resources become available to help the affected areas.

FEMA held emergency briefings for staff members as it became clear how serious Katrina would become.

to accommodate the hundreds of thousands of frantic Gulf Coast residents who were trying to leave the area before the hurricane struck.

However, many others living along the Gulf Coast didn't leave. Some had survived Hurricane Camille in 1969 and couldn't imagine that Katrina could be worse. Others wouldn't abandon their homes, pets, or spouses whose poor health prevented them from traveling. Still others didn't own cars and lacked the financial resources to purchase airfare or bus or train tickets and pay for temporary lodging elsewhere. Some who stayed headed to emergency shelters, while others stayed home and stocked up on water, non-perishable food, flashlights, and other emergency supplies in anticipation of the mammoth hurricane that was expected to strike early the next morning.

The first round of damage from Katrina came from high winds and heavy rains as the storm made landfall.

Chapter 4
Katrina Explodes over the Gulf Coast

Hurricane Katrina made landfall as a large Category 3 hurricane at 6:10 AM on August 29 in Plaquemines **Parish**, Louisiana. The storm was third in intensity of any hurricane on record to make landfall in the United States. By 10:00 AM, Katrina made landfall near the border of Louisiana and Mississippi and plowed into Biloxi and Gulfport, Mississippi, ravaging both cities. In less than a day, the hurricane spawned dozens of tornadoes and **obliterated** entire coastal towns in Louisiana, Mississippi, and Alabama. More than1.7 million people were without power, many for several weeks.

As damaging as Katrina's powerful winds were, the accompanying **storm surge** caused staggering damage. Storm surge is an atypical rise in water level caused by the strong winds of a tropical storm. As rotating winds blow on the surface of the ocean, they cause the water level to rise beneath the strongest winds. The higher water is not a problem in open waters, but near a coastline, the presence of the ocean bottom restricts the movement of water, forcing it up and inland.

Hurricane Katrina's maximum storm surge was 31 feet (9.5 m) at Waveland, Mississippi. Along some rivers and bays on the Mississippi coast, the water **inundated** up to 12 miles (19 km) inland. Eastern Louisiana had surges between 10 and 19 feet (3–5.8 m) and Alabama between 10 and 15 feet (3–4.6 m). The severity of storm surge was attributed to the enormity of the storm, the fact that it was a Category 5 hurricane just before landfall, and the shallowness of the coastal waters.

Storm surge carried houses, cars, bridges, boats, and piers inland. It filled up houses with water and forced people into their attics. When the water continued to rise, many were overcome by the water and drowned. Others were able to break holes in their roofs and escape. People waited on

Survivor Account

Mike Spencer of Gulfport, Mississippi, ignored the evacuation order but knew he'd made a huge mistake as soon as he saw Katrina's strength on the morning of August 29. He was trapped in his beachfront home as it began to fill with water. He later recalled, "I anticipated it being bad, but not nearly as severe as it turned out. The house just filled up with water. It forced me into the attic and then I ended up kicking out the wall and climbing out to a tree." Spencer spent six or more hours in the tree until neighbors discovered him. While waiting to be rescued, he watched house after house, including his own, collapse and be carried away.

When people could not break through the roof of a flooded house, rescue workers had to cut an opening.

roofs, screaming for help, until rescuers could reach them by boat or helicopter.

When Hurricane Katrina made landfall on the morning of August 29, people in New Orleans were relieved that their city hadn't suffered a direct hit. As dire as Katrina's impact proved to be all along the Gulf Coast, New Orleans residents thought the worst had passed. They couldn't have been more wrong.

Flooding destroyed so many roads, including this big freeway interchange, that much of New Orleans was impassable.

Chapter 5

Hard-Hit New Orleans

Although the entire Gulf Coast was vulnerable to hurricane damage, New Orleans was in an especially **precarious** situation. Much of the city was built below sea level on land that was drained in the early 1900s so New Orleans could expand. At the time, workers installed artificial levees and drainage canals to protect the low-lying areas from being inundated by water. For the remainder of the twentieth century, the system was mostly effective, although extensive flooding occurred in certain areas during hurricanes in 1947 and 1965 as well as during heavy rains in 1995.

Hurricane Katrina struck New Orleans in the early hours of August 29. Storm surge caused the city's levee system to become strained and eventually fail, which caused catastrophic flooding throughout 80 percent of the city and nearby areas. Rescue efforts, hampered by a lack of power and communications, were slow, leaving thousands trapped for days in homes, on roofs, and in **perilous** emergency shelters without food, water, or **sanitation**. At least 700 people in New Orleans alone lost their lives, more than 400,000 were **displaced**, and roughly 134,000 homes were badly damaged or destroyed.

Early Warnings

On August 27, Hurricane Katrina was barreling toward the Gulf Coast, and a federal state of emergency in Louisiana had already been declared. New Orleans Mayor Ray Nagin took the threat of disaster seriously. With Katrina expected to strike within thirty-six hours, he called for a voluntary evacuation of New Orleans. He also announced the possibility of a mandatory evacuation. At a news conference at 4:00 PM that day, Nagin stated, "Ladies and gentlemen, this is not a test. This is the real deal. Board up your homes, make sure you have enough medicine, make sure the car has

Survivor Account

Jourdan Froeba's family left New Orleans for Gulf Breeze, Florida, the day before Katrina struck. The drive, which typically took four hours, instead took 13 hours because of the evacuation traffic. Froeba later wrote, "We stayed at my aunt's house along with 32 other relatives who evacuated for the storm . . . almost 50 people and nine animals staying in a four-bedroom, two-bathroom house." Another New Orleans resident recalled an 11-hour drive to reach her sister's apartment in Baton Rouge, Louisiana. "Despite the 16 people staying in the three-bedroom condo, I remember celebrating our arrival. It was a hurricane party, until we awoke six hours later to the destruction that would affect our lives forever."

People left by train and bus after Mayor Ray Nagin (right) ordered the evacuation of New Orleans.

enough gas. Do all things you normally do for a hurricane but treat this one differently because it is pointed towards New Orleans."

The next day, Nagin imposed a mandatory evacuation, ordering everyone in New Orleans—roughly 450,000 people and another million in the surrounding suburbs—to leave immediately. He said, "We are facing a storm that most of us have long feared. The storm surge will most likely topple our levee system." That was the day when meteorologist Robert Ricks of the National Weather Service issued the "doomsday alert," which predicted that Katrina would be a hurricane of catastrophic proportions.

The Superdome, a stadium where thousands took shelter, had its roof battered by Katrina.

Ricks later said he had looked for statements to leave out of the warning, but he couldn't find any because they were all valid. As a native of New Orleans, he'd been through severe hurricanes, particularly Betsy (1965) and Camille (1969). Ricks knew that residents of the city had been expecting a calamitous hurricane for many years. Although he hoped Katrina wasn't "the big one," indications suggested otherwise.

Most of New Orleans' residents evacuated, but roughly 150,000 stayed behind. Many lived in poverty and lacked the money to leave. Others were elderly, ill, or disabled. Mayor Nagin opened the Louisiana Superdome as an emergency shelter, and National Guard members delivered enough bottled water and packaged meals for 15,000 people for three days. At least twice as many people ended up staying there for six days, with tragic results.

The Deluge

Hurricane Katrina severely battered New Orleans and caused widespread destruction. Rain fell as fast as one inch (2.5 cm) per hour, and strong winds blew out windows and tore the roofs off of buildings. Storm surge poured into Lake Pontchartrain, north of the city, **overtopping** many of the lake's levees and flooding communities with up to 19 feet (5.8 m) of water. More than 50 floodwalls and levees failed to protect New Orleans, some from overtopping and others because they were not anchored deeply enough in the ground and collapsed or washed away when the earth gave way.

The most significant breaches were located along three canals. A 30-foot (9 m) section of floodwall along the 17th Street Canal failed, quickly widening to 450 feet (137 m) and causing the Lakeview neighborhood to flood. Two sections of floodwall along the London Avenue Canal failed, which caused the Gentilly neighborhood to flood. The Lower Ninth Ward, located along the Industrial Canal, became completely submerged when sections of the floodwall failed, opening a 1,000-foot (305 m) gap. Those breaches also flooded St. Bernard Parish and, combined with floodwaters from the other two canals, caused 80 percent of New Orleans to become submerged, some areas with up to 20 feet (6 m) of water.

Survivor Account

Kaycie Leillah Gautreaux was six when Katrina hit New Orleans. After the hurricane passed through, Kaycie thought everything would be okay until the flooding began. "That was when we who survived were forced to sit on rooftops and wait for someone to come rescue us. I think I sat on that roof for two days, baking in the hot Louisiana sun." A helicopter finally rescued her. Kaycie now lives with her aunt in Tennessee. She lost her parents and three brothers in the hurricane.

Experts predicted the possibility of storm surge over-topping some of New Orleans' floodwalls and levees, but they didn't anticipate those structures breaking. Engineers later admitted that the system was not designed to hold up against a hurricane as strong as Katrina.

As a result of the flooding, thousands of people were trapped on rooftops and in attics. Many others didn't even have time to attempt to reach safety. Hundreds of bodies of drowning victims were later recovered from the areas hardest hit by the flooding. More than 200,000 homes were destroyed, and the city experienced a massive power outage.

New Orleans was also without drinking water because of a broken **water main**. Doctors and nurses at hospitals worked frantically, and often unsuccessfully, around the clock to save the lives of patients dependent on machines that relied on electricity and clean water until those patients could be transferred to other hospitals.

Military helicopters dropped sandbags to try to hold back the water after levees broke. Each sandbag weighed thousands of pounds.

Most cell phones were out of service because of the power outage, line breaks, and equipment damage. Roads in the majority of New Orleans were submerged, and most of the main roads into and out of the city were badly damaged. Dozens of segments of the I-10 Twin Span Bridge, near the east end of Lake Pontchartrain, were completely dislodged and hundreds of others misaligned. The lack of available routes, along with the interruption in communications, severely hindered rescue efforts.

Survivor Account

Bob Moeinian is responsible for all drainage and sewerage pumping for the city of New Orleans. On August 28, 2005, he and four other operators were stationed at the I-10 Drainage Pumping Station, prepared to work through the hurricane. By midday on August 29, water started rising all around, eventually flooding the pumping stations, damaging the equipment. All affected equipment was immediately shut down, and workers at the affected facilities had to do whatever they could to survive. Some were trapped at the stations for more than 48 hours.

Bob's family had evacuated the night before Katrina struck, but like many others, he lost his home and cars. Bob recalled the effort to get the equipment working and drain the city in the days that followed. "Seeing workers from all walks of life come together for a common cause, in this case defending the city of New Orleans, was inspiring. Additionally, the fact that they had no homes left and came back to work hard to get the system up and running was even more inspiring to me."

People in Crisis

The flooding, along with the loss of power, communications, and roads, paralyzed New Orleans and made it impossible for the people most at risk to get help. By August 30, at least 100,000 people were desperate. About 30,000 were in the Superdome, and 20,000 were in the Ernest N. Morial Convention Center. Many thousands were stranded in attics and on rooftops, and others sought safety above the floodwaters on bridges and overpasses. Governor Blanco issued an evacuation order for the entire city, and search-and-rescue efforts began, mainly by boat and helicopter.

Once Katrina had passed through, the high summer heat brought a new set of problems. Because of the power outage, food spoiled quickly and air conditioning was

People waited on rooftops, some for days, for rescue by boat or helicopter.

29

The National Guard brought sturdy trucks that were able to get supplies through the floodwaters.

unavailable. Indoor temperatures soared, and the lack of drinking water quickly put many lives at risk. People became increasingly distraught as the dangers of **dehydration**, starvation, and lack of medical care intensified. Many died while waiting for help.

Those who headed to the city's emergency shelters walked through putrid brown floodwaters laden with gasoline, raw sewage, and toxic chemicals. Food and bottled water at the Superdome ran out quickly because twice the expected number of people sought shelter there. On August 30, the air conditioning failed, and then the power, which left people in complete darkness. The following day, the plumbing failed, and toilets soon overflowed, causing an unbearable stench. In addition, gunshots were fired and rumors of violence spread. Although conditions were horrific, people had nowhere else to go while they waited for buses to transport them to shelters in other cities. The situation was similar in the convention center, which became a second emergency shelter.

Relatives in other parts of the country were frantic with concern for stranded family members. People around the world watched the unfolding tragedy in New Orleans on television. Shocking images of thousands of disaster victims, mainly poor African Americans, caused people to wonder how such misery could happen in one of the wealthiest countries in the world.

Survivor Account

Water was filling the home of Gerald Martin, age 76, when he awoke from a nap on August 29. He grabbed some water and retreated to his attic, where he was trapped for 16 days in high heat and humidity. Floodwaters finally receded enough for him to descend to the ground floor, but he was trapped there for another two days because his house was still surrounded by water. Martin was without food for the entire time, and his water supply ran out the day before he was rescued by boat by two firefighters, who cheered when they discovered someone alive inside his house. They had spent 12 days checking homes for trapped people, and Martin was the first person they had found alive.

The Kindness of Strangers

As efforts were launched to rescue those stranded by the flooding, stories of extreme kindness and generous assistance amid the misery emerged. A teenage boy who was unable to swim overcame his fear to help 12 friends and family members, along with seven pets, through floodwaters up to their necks to reach safety. When medical equipment failed, nurses kept comatose patients alive by

Survivor Account

A Katrina survivor and her family evacuated from New Orleans to Houston. She later recalled, "After enduring a seemingly endless trek to Texas and helplessly viewing the destruction of our wonderful city on the news once we got there, it was hard for anyone affected by the storm to feel anything but total despair. But the people of Houston really went a long way toward making us feel welcome and helping us in more ways than we ever expected." In a store, a cashier was checking the mother's driver's license and noticed that the family was from New Orleans. "After offering some heartfelt words of sympathy and comfort, she gave us her cell number and urged us to call her if we needed anything. The fact that a complete stranger would offer assistance like that was astonishing. Those kind gestures from all those wonderful people made it possible for us to endure that life-altering debacle we call Hurricane Katrina."

manually pumping air into their lungs. Local police officers and firefighters rescued many people stranded on roofs by boat, as did oil refinery workers, who took boats from boat yards. Maintenance workers transported sick and disabled people with forklifts. Many of these people had flooded homes and missing family members, yet they set aside their own concerns to help others.

Assistance also poured in from other places around the country. Coast Guard and other military pilots rescued many thousands by helicopter. Emergency workers also came to help rescue people trapped in attics or on rooftops as well as to treat patients. Many also brought medical supplies to donate to clinics. Offers of aid also came from 90 member countries of the United Nations.

Over a period of several days, buses finally took evacuees from New Orleans streets and shelters to emergency shelters in other locations both within and outside of Louisiana. Individuals, churches, and organizations pro-vided food, clothing, and bedding to evacuees. Strangers freely donated money and various items to people who had escaped New Orleans. A family pulled into a motel parking lot in Texas where evacuees were rumored to be staying and unloaded an enormous supply of groceries, bottled water, diapers, and toiletries from their car. In San Antonio, an airline employee gave her shoes to a barefoot evacuee.

Saving the Animals

In addition to the people whose lives were in crisis because of Katrina, roughly 250,000 pets were stranded by the storm and flooding. People who evacuated New Orleans expected to be gone for only a few days and were advised to leave four days' worth of water and food for their pets. Emergency shelters did not allow pets, so people had no choice but to leave them behind or let them loose. When owners' absences lengthened into weeks, dogs, cats, birds, and other animals were left to fend for themselves without the love and care of the people they depended upon.

Thousands of animal rescue volunteers from around the country converged on New Orleans to help the stranded animals. They braved toxic floodwaters and broke into locked and shuttered homes to coax sick, frightened animals into crates. They also roamed neighborhoods to try to capture **traumatized** animals that were running free. Many animals were badly injured as well as severely dehydrated and **malnourished**. Most of the rescued animals were taken to an emergency animal shelter set up at the Lamar-Dixon Expo Center, a large fairgrounds outside of New Orleans, where they received emergency care and where volunteers recorded their original location, breed, sex, and other information. Many animals were later transported to shelters in other states and were listed in an

Volunteers were able to rescue this dog and about 15,000 other pets that owners had to leave behind.

online database in hopes of locating their owners. Some were successfully reunited, and those whose owners couldn't be identified were placed in foster care or found new homes. The effort to rescue the pets stranded by Katrina may be the largest animal rescue operation ever conducted. Even so, thousands of animals perished.

For many people, being separated from their pets was as heartbreaking as the devastation that New Orleans itself experienced. In 2006, in response to the situation, the United States passed a law requiring the Federal Emergency Management Agency (FEMA) to ensure that emergency disaster plans address the needs of people with pets and service animals.

Animals besides pets were also impacted by the hurricane. Most of the 10,000 fish in New Orleans' Aquarium of the Americas died when the city lost power and workers had to evacuate. Workers destroyed the aquarium's piranhas to prevent them from escaping and breeding in the wild. Animals that survived the power failure, including penguins, birds, sea otters, and sea dragons, were temporarily transported to facilities in Texas and California.

Survivor Account

Alex Chernavsky was working at an animal shelter near Rochester, New York, when Hurricane Katrina hit. He went to New Orleans to join the animal rescue effort. Alex helped with search-and-rescue missions, working with another volunteer to help retrieve animals, mainly dogs and cats. They carried sledgehammers, crowbars, and other tools that would allow them to break into the houses of residents who had been evacuated but who were forced to leave their pets behind. Recalling his time in New Orleans, Alex said, "The work was physically and emotionally difficult, but I was proud to be part of a team of dedicated animal lovers who cooperated in saving as many animals as we could. I grieve for the animals who died despite our best efforts, but I'm also gratified by the lives we saved. I look back upon this experience as one of the most memorable and important things I've accomplished in my life."

Surviving the Disaster

New Orleans was in crisis on many fronts, and help from official sources was slow. Without power, communications, or roads, rescue workers had limited means to come to the aid of the thousands of people who urgently needed help. An additional aspect of the crisis was widespread rumors about looting and violence. Many situations reported as looting were stranded survivors who took water, food, and other items essential for survival. Beyond that, reports of robberies, murders, riots, and other violence spread, heightening the atmosphere of panic and desperation. Some rescue workers reported being shot at. In the midst of the chaos, along with the worsening situations in the Superdome and convention center, many people criticized federal, state, and local governments for failing to effectively address the **escalating** emergency.

On September 1, Mayor Nagin pleaded for assistance from the federal government. The next day, thousands of National Guard troops arrived, along with supply trucks, and thousands more came within the next few days. In addition, buses were sent to evacuate people from the city, and U.S. Navy ships arrived to rescue people still stranded by the floodwaters. By September 3, order had been restored, and assistance from governments, organizations, and other sources had increased.

It took weeks for drainage pumps to clear New Orleans of the foul, contaminated **water.**

On September 6, Mayor Nagin ordered a forced evacuation of all people who were still in the city in light of health and safety concerns. Once all residents had been evacuated, emergency workers faced the bleak task of recovering the bodies of people who had died.

The day after the levee and floodwall breaches, operators at the pumping stations discovered that some of the equipment was not seriously damaged. With help from the U.S. Army Corps of Engineers, the local power company, and other companies, they were able to get a few pumps at selected facilities up and running. Those pumps ultimately drained the city, but additional flooding occurred one month later when Hurricane Rita struck the Gulf Coast. New Orleans was finally declared free of floodwaters on October 11.

Many organizations temporarily provided food, bottled water, medical care, clothing, and other necessities to residents. Others began the massive tasks of cleaning up the city, counseling traumatized people, assisting with employment, and rebuilding homes. Thousands of people were still living in temporary housing five years later. New Orleans and its people are still working to recover from Hurricane Katrina's devastation.

Leaving New Orleans

More than 400,000 people evacuated New Orleans because of Hurricane Katrina. They left with few possessions and no idea when they would be able to return. Many evacuees who were scattered across the country decided not to come back. They had lost their homes, possessions, and livelihoods, and government assistance with recovery was slow in coming. The population of New Orleans was about 450,000 when Katrina struck. The following year, the population plummeted to about 223,000. In 2013, it was back up to about 360,000, with some former residents returning and people from other parts of the country relocating there.

Katrina left behind more than flooding and destruction.
As the Gulf Coast continues to recover, lessons learned
in 2005 are being applied.

Chapter 6
Katrina's Aftermath and Legacy

Hurricane Katrina was among the deadliest hurricanes in the history of the United States. According to the National Hurricane Center, approximately 1,200 people along the Gulf Coast lost their lives, and damages totaled about $108 billion.

Katrina's economic impact was enormous, not only in the affected areas but also with regard to the U.S. economy as a whole. Beyond repairs and reconstruction, more than 240,000 people along the Gulf Coast lost their jobs, and thousands of businesses were destroyed. In addition, companies that relied on tourism suddenly had no customers.

Oil production in the six months following Katrina dropped to about one-quarter of its normal rate because of damage to oil platforms and refineries, which resulted in shortages as well as high gasoline prices. Forestland was destroyed, which harmed the timber industry, and both commercial and recreational fishing were impacted by damage to boats and storage facilities as well as fish species and habitats.

Survivor Account

When the New Orleans Saints played in the 2010 Super Bowl, stories about Katrina were in the news. Teresia Schimmel saw a cousin's social networking post about being tired of hearing about Katrina. Schimmel later wrote, "To her, and many others in other states, the storm was over and life was completely back to normal here. Most of us have indeed gotten back to our lives. But please don't anyone think that it didn't affect us. And when we went to that Super Bowl in 2010, it ... brought back a confidence and pride in this city that some of us had forgotten after the storm. So, when you see a story about a city ... that is digging its way out of the ashes, feel a little pride right along with them, regardless of if it has been five years since they surfaced, because there's always someone still digging."

The hurricane also caused high levels of waste products and toxic chemicals to enter the water system, particularly when New Orleans flooded, which raised concerns about toxicity in aquatic food species. Although the U.S. economy bounced back from Katrina's impact within a year, the Gulf Coast region is still in recovery mode.

About 650,000 people who lived along the Gulf Coast were displaced by Katrina, and about 217,000 homes were destroyed or badly damaged. After Katrina and Rita, more than 300,000 evacuees were still living in temporary shelters, and they were eager to begin rebuilding their lives. The Federal Emergency Management Agency (FEMA) issued emergency funds to evacuees, but many had nowhere to go because of a shortage of rental homes in the Gulf region. FEMA provided many evacuees with mobile homes, which were intended as temporary housing until damaged or destroyed homes could be repaired or rebuilt. However, for many people, the cost of repairing or rebuilding was simply too high. As of January 2015, 76,000 FEMA mobile homes were still occupied by survivors of Hurricanes Katrina and Rita. Concerns have arisen about the mobile homes being a health hazard because of high levels of formaldehyde, a dangerous chemical, in the materials.

Some people along the Gulf Coast were not eligible for government assistance after Katrina because of their higher income level. Many were unable to collect on insurance policies because they had not purchased separate policies to cover flood damage. Regardless of their means, people who lived along Katrina's path were hard hit financially, and many are still struggling to make ends meet and figure out how to move forward in their lives.

FEMA brought in trailers to house displaced people. A typical trailer has room for two adults and two kids.

Learning from Katrina

Hurricane Katrina raised many questions about how government agencies prepare for disasters and respond to them. Much of the suffering caused by Katrina happened because government response was slow and because people who were in crisis had to wait for days to get help.

Several months after Katrina, President Bush issued a report about lessons learned from the disaster. Among the lessons was an acknowledgment that "Hurricane Katrina and the subsequent sustained flooding of New Orleans exposed significant flaws in our national preparedness for catastrophic events and our capacity to respond to them." The report identified the importance of developing a national preparedness system and ensuring that the mistakes made during Hurricane Katrina are not repeated. Government agencies mobilized much more efficiently when Hurricane Rita struck the Gulf Coast less than a month later.

For governments at all levels, Hurricane Katrina was a wakeup call. For many of the people directly affected, the storm was a harrowing challenge that also proved to be inspiring. Katrina survivor Caitlin Rotherham later recalled, "When I think about Hurricane Katrina, I will forever think about the kindness of other people in times of need. It's when you think you have absolutely nothing that the kindness of others shows through."

Both trained rescuers and ordinary people with boats helped Katrina survivors get to safety. More than 30,000 were rescued by boat.

Glossary

calamitous Causing great harm or suffering.

catastrophic Involving or causing a tremendous amount of damage.

contaminated Being dangerous or dirty because of the presence of one or more polluting, poisonous, or otherwise harmful substances.

dehydration The state of being without sufficient water for the body to function properly.

devastated Caused ruin.

displaced Forced to leave one's home.

escalating Becoming more serious, intense, or problematic.

evacuation The act of removing people from a dangerous area.

harrowing Extremely distressing.

inundated Covered with an enormous amount of water; flooded.

landfall The arrival of a hurricane over land.

levee A raised bank or wall built to prevent flooding.

malnourished Suffering as a result of lack of food or lack of healthy food.

mandatory Required by laws or rules.

meteorologist A scientist who is trained to study weather and Earth's atmosphere.

obliterated Destroyed completely.

overtopping Exceeding the height of.

parish An area of land in Louisiana that is the equivalent to a county in other states.

perilous Involving great danger.

precarious Risky; unsafe.

sanitation Services aimed at keeping places free of dirt and infection through the removal of waste, garbage, and trash.

storm surge An atypical rise in water level along a body of water caused by a tropical storm's strong winds.

sustained Relatively long lasting.

traumatized Subject to lasting upset as a result of an intensely disturbing experience.

water main A large underground pipe in a water supply system.

For More Information

Books

Andrekson, Judy. *Gunner: Hurricane Horse*.
Toronto, ON, Canada: Tundra Books, 2010.

Miller, Debra. *Hurricane Katrina: Devastation on the Gulf Coast*.
Farmington Hills, MI: Lucent Books, 2006.

Tarshis, Lauren. *I Survived #3: I Survived Hurricane Katrina, 2005*.
New York, NY: Scholastic, Inc., 2011.

Websites

Because of the changing nature of Internet links, Rosen Publishing has
developed an online list of websites related to the subject of this book. This
site is updated regularly. Please use this link to access this list:

http://www.rosenlinks.com/SD/Katrina

Index